WAKING UP SOBER

A Gentle Guide to Recovery from Alcohol

Rocky Bottoms

Vegas Nerve Productions

VEGAS NERVE
PRODUCTIONS

Cover design by: Rocky Bottoms
ISBN:978-1-7325323-7-3
Printed in the United States of America

For the one still struggling in silence--
may this light find you in the dark

The road back to yourself is the longest you'll ever walk--and the most sacred

ROCKY BOTTOMS

CONTENTS

INTRODUCTION

The Root Story

.

Before I wrote Vegas Nerves (Double Double Trouble)—a book about my recovery from compulsive gambling—I had already been through something much harder.

I got sober.

Long before I sat down to write about slot machines, sports betting, and the chaos of chasing the next win, I had walked the longer, lonelier road of alcohol and drug addiction. And I had come out the other side. Not untouched, not unscarred—but awake. Alive. Free.

That recovery became the ground I stood on when everything else started falling apart again. When gambling came for me with its neon promises and slow-motion destruction, I didn't build a brand-new path. I followed the same instincts I'd developed in sobriety: honesty over hiding. Surrender over control. Showing up, day after day, even when the sky felt empty.

This book is a return to that root story. The first victory. The one that taught me what healing really means.

I'm not writing this as a clinician, a guru, or someone with a formula. I'm writing this as a person who almost didn't make it—and did. A person who drank to forget, to feel, to disappear. A person who lied, broke promises, and woke up afraid. A person who one day said, enough—and meant it.

This book is for anyone who's still stuck in that loop. Anyone who keeps waking up with regret in their throat and wondering if it will ever change. It can. It does. But not through willpower alone.

Recovery is less like a ladder and more like a spiral. You come back to the same places again and again, but each time with a little more clarity, and a little more courage. You don't have to believe in yourself right now. Just believe in this: change is possible.

I'm not here to tell you what to do. I'm here to walk beside you as you do what you already know deep down you're meant to do. Whether this is your first day sober, your tenth relapse, or your silent cry for help—this book is for you.

Let's begin where it really began.

CHAPTER 1: WHAT IS ALCOHOL DOING TO ME?

If you're reading this, there's a part of you that knows something isn't right.

Maybe you can't stop drinking once you start. Maybe you tell yourself every morning that today will be different, only to find yourself pouring another one by nightfall. Maybe you've been hiding it. Minimizing it. Maybe people around you have started to say things—softly at first, then louder.

And maybe you've started to wonder: Is this a problem?
Let me answer that for you as simply and directly as I can:
If you're asking that question, it probably is.

That doesn't mean you're broken. It doesn't mean you're weak. It means that alcohol—this socially sanctioned, widely celebrated substance—has quietly taken more from you than you thought it could. And now you're here, asking for something different.

That's not a failure. That's the beginning.

When I was drinking, I didn't think I had a problem either. I thought I had bad luck, a stressful job, or a personality that just liked to go a little too hard. I told myself a thousand small lies. I laughed off the blackouts. I shrugged off the shame. I told people I was fine.

But alcohol was doing something to me—slowly, steadily, and without my consent. It was making my world smaller. It was dulling my joy, shrinking my courage, and stealing my mornings. It was turning my nervous system into a war zone. It was making me forget who I was.

Maybe it's doing that to you, too.

And yet, we keep drinking. Not because we're reckless or stupid, but because somewhere along the line, alcohol became the answer. The answer to anxiety, loneliness, boredom, fear. It became a bridge to connection, to sleep, to silence.

Until it stopped working. Until it started hurting.

That's where real recovery begins—not with punishment, not with guilt, but with the slow, clear realization that alcohol isn't helping anymore. That it's costing more than it's giving. That it's taking the life you actually want to live.

If you're feeling that—if something inside you knows

it's time—you're already farther along than you think. You don't have to fix everything today. You don't have to map out the next year or even the next week.

You just have to listen. And trust that the part of you reading these words—the part that still believes in another way—is right.

You're not alone. You're not beyond hope. You're at the edge of something honest.

CHAPTER 2: THE MOMENT OF TURNING

There's a quiet moment in recovery that often gets overlooked.

It's not dramatic. It doesn't always come with rock bottom or flashing lights. Sometimes it happens in the middle of folding laundry. Or driving. Or staring at the ceiling at 3 a.m. It's the moment you whisper to yourself—not out loud, not even fully formed—I can't keep doing this.

That's the moment of turning.

It may not feel like much at first. You might still drink tomorrow. You might still lie to yourself next week. But something shifts. A crack opens. Something deeper than fear begins to stir—something like clarity. Something like truth.

This isn't working.
I don't want to live like this.

There has to be another way.

When I reached that moment, it wasn't a single event. It was a slow-burning ache that finally became undeniable. I was exhausted—emotionally, spiritually, physically. I couldn't keep pretending I was okay. I couldn't keep patching my days together with hangovers and half-truths.

And I didn't know what recovery would look like. I didn't have a plan. I just knew something had to give.

That's the moment this whole journey hinges on. Not the day you quit. Not the day you get a chip or a certificate or a clean calendar. The day you stop arguing with reality. The day you start telling the truth to yourself, even just a sliver of it.

It's okay if you're scared. It's okay if you're not sure what comes next. What matters is that you've heard something inside you that can't be unheard.

You don't have to call it rock bottom. You don't even have to hit one. The idea that you have to lose everything before you get better is a myth—and a dangerous one. You don't have to go lower. You can start from right here.

And starting doesn't mean you're suddenly strong. It just means you're ready to stop lying. To stop bargaining. To stop putting it off until Monday or next year or some magical version of yourself that has it all together.

You're here now. That's enough.

Turning is not the end of the story. It's the beginning of the real one.

CHAPTER 3: EARLY SOBRIETY — THE FIRST DAYS AND WEEKS

The early days of sobriety can feel like stepping onto another planet. Everything is louder, sharper, heavier. Your body hurts. Your emotions feel like strangers. Time crawls. Sleep disappears.

You wonder if it's supposed to feel this bad.
You wonder if you're doing it wrong.
You wonder if maybe you're just not built for this.

You are.
And no, you're not doing it wrong.
This is just the beginning, and beginnings are messy.

When I first got sober, I thought it would feel like a triumph. Instead, it felt like grief. I wasn't just losing alcohol; I was losing a way of life. I was losing my favorite coping tool, my security blanket, my way to avoid myself. I had to face everything I'd been trying to drown out—and it hit all at once.

If you're feeling that too, I want you to know: it's normal.
It's temporary.
And it's survivable.

Here's what you might experience in early sobriety:

- Physical symptoms like shaking, sweating, headaches, nausea, insomnia, and exhaustion. (If you are experiencing severe withdrawal symptoms like hallucinations, seizures, or extreme confusion, seek medical help immediately. Detoxing from alcohol can be dangerous without support.)
- Emotional whiplash—crying one minute, laughing the next, raging the next. Think of it like thawing out after being frozen for a long time. The feeling is messy at first.
- Mental chatter—your mind may race, bargain, plead. You may hear that seductive voice: Was it really that bad? You can handle one or two. Maybe this time will be different.
- Profound boredom—the hours seem endless when they aren't soaked in alcohol. You may feel restless, empty, and unsure of what to do with yourself.

All of this is normal. All of it passes.

Not quickly. Not cleanly. But it passes.

In the first few days, your only job is this: don't drink today.

Don't worry about forever. Don't worry about next month or your next birthday or Christmas or weddings or barbecues. Don't drown yourself in a thousand future fears. Stay where your feet are. Stay in this one day.

And if a whole day feels too big?
Break it down to an hour. Or a minute. Or a breath.

Early sobriety is not about feeling good. It's about staying alive and staying awake. It's about not making today harder by chasing yesterday's habits.

You don't have to be strong. You just have to be willing.

You don't have to figure it all out. You just have to trust that even the worst hour will pass without you picking up a drink.

That is your superpower now: getting through the next feeling, the next craving, the next uncomfortable minute.

That's how sobriety is built—not by giant leaps of transformation, but by a thousand tiny acts of staying.

And one day soon, you'll wake up and realize:
It's a little less dark.
It's a little less heavy.
It's a little more possible.

You are not failing because it's hard.
You are succeeding because you're still here.

CHAPTER 4: WHAT HELPS — AND WHAT DOESN'T

In early sobriety, everyone has advice.

Some of it will help. Some of it won't.
You'll hear slogans, programs, books, podcasts, promises. You'll hear about the one thing that "saved" someone else. You'll hear about what you "have to do" or you'll "never make it."

Breathe.
Take what you need. Leave the rest.

Recovery isn't one-size-fits-all. It's a living, breathing process. You get to build it, piece by piece, in the way that fits your mind, your heart, and your life.

That said, some things tend to help a lot of people—and some traps that can quietly sabotage you without you even realizing it.

What Helps

1. Connection.
Isolation fuels addiction. Find someone to talk to—a group, a sponsor, a therapist, a friend who gets it. You don't have to bare your soul on day one. Just start letting yourself be seen.

2. Structure.
Chaos invites relapse. Early sobriety thrives on simple, steady routines: when you wake up, when you eat, when you sleep, when you move your body. Create rhythm where there used to be chaos.

3. Honesty.
Lying to others is easy. Lying to yourself is deadly. Keep it simple: I'm struggling. I'm scared. I don't know what I'm doing. Honesty isn't weakness—it's the scaffolding for the new life you're building.

4. Safe places.
Bars, parties, old drinking buddies—these might not be your best environment for a while. Permit yourself to protect your early recovery like you would protect a broken bone. Healing needs safety.

5. Tiny goals.
Don't aim for "forever sober" in one leap. Aim for today. For this afternoon. For this hour. Small victories stack up, and they matter more than you know.

6. Self-forgiveness.
You'll mess up. You'll snap at people. You'll feel all over the place. Good. That means you're alive and healing. Don't punish yourself for not being perfect. Recovery is a human thing, not a heroic one.

What Doesn't Help

1. Relying on willpower alone.
White-knuckling works... until it doesn't. Recovery is not about gritting your teeth harder—it's about changing your relationship with yourself, your feelings, and your coping tools.

2. Playing the comparison game.
Someone else got sober faster. Someone else seems happier. Someone else had a bigger rock bottom. None of it matters. You are not them. You are you. Stay in your lane.

3. "Testing yourself."
The voice that says "Maybe I can just have one now" is not your friend. Early sobriety isn't the time for experiments. Protect it like it's fragile—because it is.

4. All-or-nothing thinking.
If you slip, it doesn't mean you've lost everything. You don't have to blow up your progress because of one bad night. Guilt will tell you to give up. Grace will tell you to

get up.

You don't have to do all the right things.
You don't have to do them perfectly.
You just have to stay close to yourself—your real self—the one that's trying, the one that showed up today, the one that picked up this book.

That part of you is strong enough.
You're strong enough.

CHAPTER 5: THE WALL AND THE BREAKTHROUGH

The first days and weeks of sobriety are brutal.
And then—sometimes—they get better.
You start waking up without a hangover. You remember conversations. You feel a flicker of pride you haven't felt in years.

And then, out of nowhere, you slam into The Wall.

It's a real thing. Almost everyone in recovery hits it at some point.

The Wall is that sudden crash of fatigue, sadness, boredom, anger, or loneliness that makes you think:
I can't do this.
I don't even want to do this.
Is this all there is?

It's sneaky because it shows up after you've had some success. After you've had enough time away from alcohol to start feeling... something. And when it hits, it can feel like you're back at the beginning.

You're not.
Hitting the Wall doesn't mean you're failing.
It means you're about to break through something deeper.

Why the Wall Happens

Alcohol wasn't just a problem.
It was a solution—for pain, for anxiety, for emptiness. It was a shortcut to feeling better (or at least feeling less). When you take it away, the problems it covered up are still there, waiting.

You start to feel the old fears. The unresolved grief. The loneliness. The disappointments. The rawness of life, without a buffer.

This is the part of sobriety where a lot of people think: Maybe drinking wasn't my problem after all. Maybe it was my life.

They're not wrong.

But the answer isn't to go back to drinking.
The answer is to keep going through.

Because what's on the other side of the Wall isn't just more sobriety. It's your actual life. Your real self. Not the numbed-out version. Not the edited version. The whole, breathing, messy, beautiful thing.

How to Get Through It

1. Name it.
If you feel trapped, hopeless, or miserable—say so. Speak it out loud. Tell someone. The Wall feeds on silence. Breaking that silence weakens it.

2. Lower the bar.
When you hit the Wall, basic survival counts as success. Showering counts. Eating a sandwich counts. Going to bed without drinking counts. You don't have to thrive—you just have to stay upright.

3. Change the channel.
When your mind is screaming for relief, distract it if you can. Walk. Watch a stupid movie. Call someone. Listen to music. Sobriety isn't just about facing pain—it's also about learning to shift your energy when you need to.

4. Remember: it's temporary.
No feeling, no craving, no dark mood lasts forever. They rise. They peak. They fall. The Wall feels eternal while you're inside it, but it isn't. Hold on. It will shift.

You don't have to love sobriety every day.
You don't have to feel grateful every second.
You just have to keep moving forward, even when every part of you wants to turn back.

Because on the other side of the Wall, there's something no drink can ever give you:
A life you actually want to stay awake for.

And you are already closer than you think.

CHAPTER 6: BUILDING A LIFE YOU DON'T WANT TO ESCAPE FROM

Sobriety isn't just about quitting drinking.
It's about creating a life that feels too good to numb.

At first, you're just surviving. One day at a time, one craving at a time. It's hard, raw, and exhausting.
But something strange starts to happen the longer you stay sober: you begin to care about your life again.

You start to see spaces where there used to be only walls.
You start to imagine possibilities instead of punishments.
You start to realize: I'm not just here to not drink. I'm here to live.

That's when real recovery begins.

What Makes Life Worth Staying For?

You don't have to overhaul your whole world overnight. But you do have to ask yourself some questions you might not have dared to ask in years:

- What lights me up, even a little?
- What kind of people make me feel more like myself?
- What places, routines, and activities feel nourishing instead of numbing?
- What did I love—or even just like—before drinking took over?
- What am I curious about now?

Your answers don't have to be dramatic. You don't have to move to a cabin in the woods or become a marathon runner or find your "one true passion."
You just have to start noticing.

Recovery isn't about becoming someone new. It's about remembering who you were before alcohol convinced you that you weren't enough.

It's about slowly, bravely, building a life you don't need to hide from.

Some Building Blocks for a Sober Life

1. Creativity.
Painting, writing, singing, gardening, woodworking, cooking—anything that lets you make something instead of just consuming.

2. Movement.
Not punishment. Not shame. Just moving your body in a way that feels good: walks, yoga, dancing alone in your living room.

3. Connection.
Real conversations. Honest laughter. Friendships that aren't built around a bottle. People who see you, not your drinking persona.

4. Learning.
Books, classes, podcasts, new skills. Feeding your mind instead of numbing it.

5. Rest.
Not the frantic, crash-on-the-couch kind. The real kind—sleeping enough, slowing down, treating yourself like a living being, not a machine.

6. Purpose.
It doesn't have to be grand. It could be raising your kids, caring for your dog, planting a garden, helping others in recovery, or just showing up for your own life with honesty.

When drinking was the center of your life, it dictated your priorities, your choices, and your relationships. Now, you get to decide what fills that space.

And even if you don't know the answers yet—even if it feels overwhelming—trust this:
You are capable of creating a life that doesn't hurt to live.

You're already doing it.
Every sober day, every choice to stay awake, every act of kindness toward yourself is a brick in that foundation.

And the life you're building?
It's going to be stronger, wilder, and more beautiful than anything alcohol ever promised.

CHAPTER 7: HANDLING CRAVINGS, TRIGGERS, AND TEMPTATIONS

Recovery doesn't happen in a vacuum.

Sooner or later, real life will come knocking:
The family party where everyone's drinking.
The stressful workday that leaves you raw.
The lonely Friday night when old habits whisper.

Cravings will come.
Triggers will flare up.
Temptations will dance around, wearing a thousand disguises.

None of this means you're doing recovery wrong.
It means you're alive—and that you're learning a new way to be alive.

The trick isn't to avoid every craving, every trigger, every temptation.
The trick is to learn how to walk through them without surrendering.

Cravings: The False Alarm

A craving feels like an emergency.
Like it will never end unless you give in.
But cravings are liars.

They don't last forever. They peak and they fall, like waves.
Most cravings, even the intense ones, only last 15 to 30 minutes if you don't feed them.

When a craving hits:

- Pause.

Take a breath. Name what's happening: This is a craving. It will pass.

- Change your surroundings.

Move rooms. Step outside. Splash cold water on your face. Shifting your physical state shifts your mental one.

- Delay the decision.

Tell yourself you'll wait 10 minutes. Then 10 more. The craving will often weaken if you give it time.

- Reach out.

Text someone. Call someone. Say, “I’m having a craving and I just needed to tell someone.” Saying it out loud cuts its power in half.

Triggers: Old Roads to Nowhere

A trigger is anything that wakes up the old pathways in your brain:
A certain bar. A song. A time of day. A person. A smell.

Triggers make you feel like drinking is the obvious, inevitable next step.
It’s not.

When a trigger hits:

- Acknowledge it.

Don’t pretend you’re fine if you’re not. Pretending makes it stronger. “That bar is a trigger for me.” That’s honesty, not weakness.

- Have an escape plan.

If you know you’ll be somewhere triggering (a wedding, a holiday gathering), plan ahead. Know how you’ll leave early if you need to. Know who you’ll text. Know what you’ll say if someone offers you a drink.

- Stack your defenses.

Before big triggering events, make sure you're fed, rested, and emotionally supported. HALT (Hungry, Angry, Lonely, Tired) makes triggers 10 times harder.

Temptations: The Seductive Voice

Temptation often comes disguised as logic:
Just one won't hurt.
You deserve it after today.
Maybe you're not really an alcoholic.
No one will know.

These thoughts are part of the game your addiction plays.
It's not about truth. It's about survival—your old coping mechanism trying to stay alive.

When temptation whispers:

- Answer it.

Don't argue endlessly. Just respond clearly: "Maybe so. But today, I'm staying sober."

- Play the tape forward.

Imagine the whole story, not just the first sip: the guilt, the shame, the spiraling. Is it worth it?

- Remember why you started.

Go back to your first moments of clarity. What

brought you here? What were you tired of? Anchor yourself there.

You are not powerless over cravings, triggers, or temptations.
You are learning how to live with them—and through them—without handing your life back over to a drink.

Every time you do that, you're not just surviving.
You're practicing freedom.

One decision at a time.
One hour at a time.
One breath at a time.

CHAPTER 8: WHEN YOU SLIP (AND HOW TO GET BACK UP)

Slips happen.

Not to everyone.
But to enough people that we need to talk about it.

Because shame loves silence. And if we don't talk about slipping, we set ourselves up to stay stuck if it ever happens.

Here's the truth:
A slip is not the end of your story.
It's not proof that you "can't" get sober.
It's not a reason to give up.

It's just a stumble on a very human path.

What a Slip Really Means

A slip (or relapse) doesn't erase all your progress.
It doesn't mean you wasted your sober time.
It doesn't mean sobriety isn't possible for you.

It usually means something needs more attention:

- An emotion you're avoiding
- A situation that overwhelms you
- A trigger you didn't see coming
- A coping tool you don't have yet

Slips are information, not damnation.

They are messy, painful, and humbling—but they are also teachers if you let them be.

If You Slip: What to Do

1. Stop the bleeding.
The sooner you stop, the better. You don't have to "make it count" by turning one drink into a full collapse. You can stop after one. Or after a weekend. Or after a month. Just stop.

2. Drop the shame.

You are not broken. You are not hopeless. You are human. Shame will tell you to give up. Pride will tell you to hide it. Recovery will tell you: Come back. You're still wanted.

3. Tell someone.
Tell the truth as soon as you can. Isolation makes a slip grow into something much bigger. Honesty shrinks it back down to size.

4. Get curious, not cruel.
Instead of beating yourself up, ask yourself: What was happening right before I slipped? What was I feeling? What was I telling myself? This is valuable information.

5. Rebuild right away.
Don't wait for the "perfect" time to restart. Today is good enough. Even if you feel bruised and shaken, plant your feet and start again.

If You Haven't Slipped Yet (But You're Scared You Might)

Good. Be humble about it.
Know that sobriety is not something you "win" once and then coast forever.

It's a daily practice. A daily choice.
Stay close to yourself. Stay honest. Stay supported.

And if you ever do slip, remember this:

You are allowed to return.
You are allowed to rebuild.
You are allowed to keep your story going.

Slipping doesn't disqualify you.
It just proves how much you still want to heal.

And you can.
You will.

CHAPTER 9: THE GIFTS OF SOBRIETY

When you first get sober, it's hard to imagine that anything good could come from it.
In fact, early on, it can feel like you've lost everything: your coping mechanisms, your routines, your sense of who you were.

But stay long enough, and something wild happens.
You start receiving gifts you didn't even know you were missing.

Not material gifts.
Not trophies.
Something better.

Sobriety gives you yourself.

The Gifts You Can't See Right Away

1. Clarity.
You begin to see yourself, your relationships, and your life without the fog. Decisions get simpler. Not easier—but clearer.

2. Self-respect.
Each sober day is a small, defiant act of love toward yourself. Over time, those days add up. And one morning, you realize: I trust myself again.

3. Emotional honesty.
Without numbing, you feel sadness, anger, joy, boredom, grief—all of it. And you survive it. You learn that no feeling has to own you.

4. Presence.
You actually live your moments. The small ones. The beautiful ones. The ones you used to rush through or erase.

5. Real connection.
Sobriety strips away the fake versions of you—the one who needed alcohol to fit in, impress, seduce, or survive. What's left is the real you. And real you connects with real people.

6. Freedom.
You don't have to check how much is left in the bottle. You don't have to lie. You don't have to hide. You don't have to lose days, nights, memories, jobs, or relationships anymore.

7. Creativity.
Life starts becoming less about managing your addiction and more about creating—art, friendships, adventures, and dreams. You reclaim your power to build something new.

Why the Gifts Are Worth the Fight

You might still have cravings sometimes.
You might still feel lost sometimes.
You might still ache for old comforts sometimes.

That's okay.
Sobriety doesn't promise a life without struggle.
It promises a life worth struggling for.

You get the hard days—but you also get the real laughter.
The deep sleep.
The honest tears.
The morning you wake up proud.
The night you fall asleep peacefully.

You get your future back.
You get your heart back.
You get your life back.

Sobriety isn't a punishment.

It's a homecoming.

Not to some perfect, polished version of yourself.
To your true self—the one who was strong enough to reach for healing even when it hurt.

And if you're reading this now, you're already well on your way home.

CHAPTER 10: RECOVERY AS A WAY OF LIFE

Somewhere along the way, sobriety stops feeling like a sentence.
It starts feeling like a path.

A way of being.
A way of living.
A way of relating to yourself and the world that is deeper, truer, and more alive than anything you knew before.

Recovery isn't just something you do anymore.
It's something you are.

More Than Not Drinking

Early on, it's all about not drinking.
Counting days. Dodging triggers. Fighting cravings.

Surviving.

But with time, something shifts:
You realize recovery isn't mainly about alcohol at all.

It's about becoming whole.
It's about learning how to meet life on life's terms.
It's about building resilience, patience, trust, honesty, and love—from the inside out.

Sobriety is the doorway.
Recovery is the journey through it.

Living Recovery, Day by Day

You don't graduate from recovery.
You grow in it.

You practice:

- Showing up even when you're tired.
- Telling the truth even when you're scared.
- Taking care of yourself even when no one's watching.
- Forgiving yourself even when you stumble.
- Choosing love over fear whenever you can.

And you keep practicing.
Not perfectly.

Not without struggle.
But with more heart, more grace, and more courage every year.

The Recovery Ripple

Your healing doesn't end with you.

When you live in recovery, you give something powerful to the people around you:

- You show that change is possible.
- You remind others that it's never too late.
- You create spaces of honesty and hope just by being yourself.

You might never know whose life you're touching, just by staying sober today.
But the ripples you create are real—and they matter.

Your Journey Continues

Recovery is not the end of the story.
It's the beginning of the story you were always meant to live.

A story with pain, yes.

But also a story with hope, love, growth, meaning, laughter, and purpose.

A story where you don't just survive.
You live.

Fully.
Bravely.
Beautifully.

You don't have to be perfect.
You just have to stay awake.
Stay honest.
Stay open.

Sobriety gave you back your life.
Recovery will teach you how to live it.

And you, my friend, are doing something extraordinary —one day at a time.

EPILOGUE

You don't need to have it all figured out.
You don't need a perfect plan.
You don't need to be fearless.

You just need one small, true step.

- Maybe it's reaching out to someone.
- Maybe it's making it through one more day sober.
- Maybe it's forgiving yourself for yesterday.
- Maybe it's choosing hope, even when it feels far away.

Whatever it is, trust that it matters.
Trust that it's enough.

Recovery isn't built in grand, sweeping moments.
It's built-in quiet, brave decisions, repeated over and over.

You are already walking your path.
You are already becoming who you were meant to be.

Your next step is waiting.

And you are ready for it.

One day.
One breath.
One beautiful life.

AFTERWORD

If you've made it this far, I want you to know something:
I am proud of you.

Not because you've done everything perfectly.
Not because you've magically erased all your struggles.

I'm proud of you because you kept going.

You made it through the nights that felt endless.
You made it through the cravings that screamed your name.
You made it through the loneliness, the doubt, the fear—and here you are, still reaching, still hoping, still alive.

That is no small thing.
That is everything.

I didn't write this book as an expert speaking down.
I wrote it as someone who knows what it feels like to

crawl out of darkness on hands and knees.

Before I ever wrote Vegas Nerves (Double Double Trouble) about gambling recovery, I lived the long, tangled path of overcoming alcohol and drug addiction. Those early lessons—the ones earned through bruises and breakthroughs—became the foundation for every other healing that followed.

I didn't always know I would make it.
I didn't always believe I deserved to.

But somewhere inside, there was a flicker that wouldn't go out.
Maybe you have that flicker too.

Hold onto it.
Protect it.
Feed it.

It's enough.

You don't have to know exactly where your path is leading.
You don't have to feel strong every step of the way.

You just have to keep moving toward the life you deserve.
The life that is already trying to find you.

From one traveler to another:
Keep going.

The world needs your sober, radiant, fierce, and beautiful heart.

And I'm rooting for you, always.

— Rocky Bottoms

Made in United States
Cleveland, OH
17 May 2026

37058600R00036